A Newfound Existence

Kenneth J Cody

ISBN: 9781710252248

A Newfound Existence

DEDICATION

This book is dedicated to my higher self the S.C. You are amazing and have helped to heal my inner soul.

This book is dedicated to the memory of my Grandmother Audrey M. Wyman Cody. I love you.

A Newfound Existence

Contents

Foreword

ACKNOWLEDGMENTS

Melissa Marie Cody, Courtney Jade Cody, Mikayla Stephanie- Lynn Cody, Caelyn Olivia- Marie Cody, Kenneth David- Keith Cody. QHHT. S.C.

A Newfound Existence

A NEWFOUND EXISTENCE

Foreword

A Newfound Existence was put together in order to explore the changes I had gone through with my personal transformation into who I am. You are going to read some of the darkest memories of mine as well as some of the more enriching moments I have experienced. This is a diverse piece of writing and I encourage you all to see where each of you stand with your own personal journey. I still have a lot of work to do but I only hope that my journey may help you along the way with yours,

Kenneth.

A Newfound Existence

1

Vehicle

Waking to smell the fresh blossoms,

The earth has gifted us,

Greeting us with its kind gesture.

Embracing our nostrils with the soothing
touch of the fall air.

We are breathing,

Therefore, we must be blessed.

Life is said to be a gift.

But to who I must ask?

When really, it's just a choice,

An adventure we must seek in order to get
to the next level.

The Earth blankets us and today makes it a little more tasteful.

For its beauty is radiating, and life is surrounding you.

Engulfed in the treasures beneath your futile being,

A vehicle to get you through this existence,

getting you to the next entry in your journey.

An overwhelming ride down the corridor to further your spot in the universe.

Elders

Memories cherished beneath the seed,

Implanted from within the inner shell of my aura.

Parental units but not by birth or construction,

Simply by nourishment and love.

Noble, wise and teaching.

An everlasting umbrella of love lingering throughout the day,

Radiating in the sun.

Forever in hopes for your life to last.

For you two were like saviors, in a world that needed saving.

A Newfound Existence

An escape from the realm of correlating
ideas,

Of punishment wrapped in discipline.

Your smile erasing the karma,

Left on those that did this creation.

Positive and negatives pursuing kinetic
energy,

And collapse in the well of further lingering
death.

Guardians of the covenant of family,

The head, elders.

Grandparents.

Poor Excuse

Hiding behind a remote.

A picture that moves in 4k.

Engulfed in the sound of Dolby

and the lingering wonder of those who care.

Forgotten? Yes? If no, then why?

Why do you choose to tuck away?

An excuse is far to petty to purify the putrid stain,

Laid upon the ground.

An elder to learn from, not wonder.

Where are you?

When you are not dead...

What will you leave onto those who carry on your flesh,

Wallowing in your shadows that no longer exist.

Not because of your parish,

But because you have chosen to no longer walk amongst them.

How will you be remembered when you have left no memories.

Silhouette

Imagine a rabid dog, only a heart is beating reminding you that your still human. My mind was racing, and it was as if all hope had been lost. I was depressed but this time it was different. I didn't understand. I had racing thoughts, clammy hands, high anxiety and extreme suicidal ideation. I was screaming inside and panting on the outside. I was in hell and unfortunately, I wasn't dreaming. I remember wanting to sleep and hating myself and dreaming of my death.

I had pictured it many of times and as I held my beautiful pistol, I knew it was not how I had planned however I felt it was my only option. I didn't want to die, but I no longer wanted to live, feeling that way. I felt as if I had lost all grip on reality, I was losing my battle with sanity.

My depressive episodes had never been this aggressive and I didn't understand, nor could I comprehend it. My racing thoughts were focusing on friends who no longer existed, the Army and what I had gone through.

I missed my childhood and I thought of my earlier suicide attempt and the failure that had followed with it. I thought that had I not failed I wouldn't be in my current nightmare. I cried and silently screamed, I smoked multiple cigarettes and tried to escape the burden of pain.

I paced around the room, the carpet beneath my feet. Why could I not sleep, if only I could to awake and breath another day. We had just learned that my ex- sister in law was pregnant with my niece Adrianna and I thought of being an uncle, I held onto everything positive to keep myself alive and as the tears poured down my cheeks the depression and the mania grew worse.

At the time I had only been diagnosed Bipolar Affective disorder and was not aware I was type 1 and that I was able to have mixed episodes, causing Dysphoric Mania.

This caused my night to grow more interesting.

I would later find out I was on the wrong medication. I laid on the bed in desperation and spoke to my grandfather who had just passed away and for whom I was very close too. He was a hero of mine and still is to this day. He was a great grandfather to me. He was always there for me and at this moment in my life I needed him more than ever. I begged my grandfather to come to me for comfort, I mean I had a gun in my lap, and was desperate, I was fighting for my life at this point.

I knew that if I could fall asleep and make it through the night, I would be here today writing my story for you to read. Soon my body grew cold and I sunk into my bed. I began to leave my room, my mania had increased, depression had subsided, and I sunk further. It was as if the gun had discharged and this was the end.

Maybe it had and God was real, I was going to Hell for my lack of faith. Soon I heard and auditory hallucination and a voice began to speak "I must get out of this place" over repeatedly. The surrounding turned green and my body began to rise.

As I began to rise, I looked to the

ceiling and saw a silhouette looking down at me of a child's face. The image was so peaceful I began to fall asleep which is all I could have ever asked for. When I awoke the next morning, the gun lay in my crotch.

Dysphoric Mania was gone fortunately as it can last long periods of time, however I was left in a depressive low episode. I survived to tell this story, and years later my daughter Mikayla was born.

She was the child in the silhouette.

2

They Come

A noise in the night,

Surrounding your ears,

beating on the drum,

No fear,

But curiosity.

A glow and a feeling.

A presence as if someone is there peering
into your safe zone.

The comforts of your resting spot.

Just enough to let you know they are there,

Collapsing at sight,

But spotted only for a moment.

Blue.

Words Hurt

The tears upon your face,

A painting I had created,

Through words with a design,

To love and to comfort.

Not to tear down.

And hurt the one for whom I love the most.

The tongue is all too powerful,

Beyond the waves of the sea.

The depths of that ocean,

And the strongest wind.

For words can destroy the shell of presence.

The inner workings of the soul,

The joy of love.

And the feeling of forgiveness.

My hurt.

My past pain,

My lack of salvation is spilling unto you.

Why?

Why after so long must you now drink from my cup.

And plunder the sheets to stay secure.

Manic Depressive Low

2003

Lately I have been in one of those zones. The lows of Manic Depression have conquered me, and I feel as that moving up is almost impossible. My veins throb and visions of slicing them open become clear. I am sad, there is no other word for it.

I feel as if in a desperate state to regain my sanity and erase the images that burn so deep inside my soul. To slowly take a gun and place it against my temple, pull the trigger and say goodbye to my life of mental anguish, self-mutilation and inner decay. I am 19 years old and feel I am all alone, like there is no cure because nothing works, and suicide is my soul mate.

I talk to my family and a friend. The pain calms and then slowly gains speed taking me full force.

Why are relationships so hard and confusing? I miss my friends; they are in Iraq and I hope they are ok. Maybe I would feel better if Cordova were here; I miss having him around to talk to. He saved my life and though I am grateful I wish I had died. I just wished that my medicine worked, and I could live happy for a while. To just hide my feelings for a day or two. And function like a normal 19-year-old man.

Soldier

June 2003

As I look at myself in my Class A uniform, I only feel one thing and that is pride. I only wish that my superiors could have been more supportive of me while going through my lows on my way out of the military. I feel guilty knowing that my friends are overseas and here I am decked out in tattoos living it up playing the Rock Star.

Hidden behind tattoos that indeed reflect my personality but do not make me who I am. Know that you are not forgotten. I will always be one of you 4/1 FA. I only wish

that the circumstances could have been

different, come home safe.

3

Dreaming of Death

There was a night where I fell fast asleep, seemingly rare I slept like a baby after having a warm bottle and on a milk drunk high. As I lay sound asleep, I felt as if I awoke to something puncturing my abdomen though I felt no pain. I could feel the pressure. I looked up and saw what looked to be doctors or medics working on my lifeless body.

I felt I had perished, and they were working to revive me. Had I dyed? Was this what it felt like when one had dyed, I mean no one truly knows until it has happened. I could see these individuals in white scrubs or gowns, with white mask upon their faces, it was both frightening and surreal. As they franticly worked to revive me, I lifted or glided out of my lifeless body.

I remember feeling a warmth and absolutely no pain, no fear, just an overwhelming sadness. An overwhelming sadness as I saw my lifeless body from above and my wife sound asleep beside it. I remember feeling sad because I wasn't able to embrace her, or my children and tell them goodbye or that I loved them. I loved them dearly and that I would miss them, I would miss them all so much and I desperately wanted to say goodbye.

I slowly began to drift down a dark tunnel, and again there was no fear. The tunnel was long, and it felt like forever to get to the end. There was a light and at the end there was an old grandmother like figure. She felt so comforting, so embracing and loving.

The first thing that came to mind and I spoke "When can I see my grandma". My Grandma had just passed and the guilt I felt for not seeing her for some time had overcome my existence. I wanted so deeply to see her and wrap my arms around her and ask for forgiveness.

Forgiveness felt as if it had been given

and I immediately woke up in tears. I no longer fear death because I have now come to realize what that dream has told me. That we live in a shell, a shape, a vehicle. We are made up of energy and are human in a sense, but our energy lives inside of our vehicle. When we pass, that energy will move on to our next journey. Death is something we should not fear, but embrace, though I am not ready for it, I will welcome it when the day comes.

Playing with an old friend

The other night I had a dream. I traveled into another dimension. I went back into time and was able to explore and hang out with an old friend. One of my best friends in Junior High or (middle school) as it is often referred to now. We hung out and it was surreal. I hadn't seen this friend since December 15, 1998, the day before Christmas break of 9th grade. Nor had I spoken to him since November Of 2001 when I was in boot camp and called random friends due to loneliness.

Traveling to another parallel

dimension is amazing. Some feel we are living multiple lives at the same time, and after many dreams such as this as well as my experience with Quantum Healing Hypnosis Technique sessions I must say I agree. Either way my experiences have been amazing.

Transcending

Transcended through the air,

A corpse beneath the energy,

The soul, the existence of recognition.

Besides oneself of glory...

And the essence of what once was the
remanence of fear.

But none of the that lingers

For sadness is all that exist.

I love you my love.

I must say goodbye,

but words cannot escape.

I'm sorry for the hurt,

Though good times remain on the horizon.

And though I will be gone,

Know there is no pain.

And fear doesn't overwhelm me.

For there is nothing to fear in death,

Just the ability to say goodbye.

Wondering

I often wonder why people look down on those around them. Do they not understand the concept of being polite and live and let live? I mean you never really know what a person could be going through and the interaction you have with that person could make or break them.

For instance, an individual could be on the brink of death and you could be the last person he or she interacts with. Or that person could be thinking about ending it all and your act of kindness steers them off the bridge.

There have been times in my life with my mood disorder that an act of kindness has boosted my mood and helped push me out of a low or pushed me further into a high. This also can happen to any individual, not just those suffering from a mental illness.

Truth be told we are all individuals who deserve love and kindness. A warm place to sleep and a meal in our bellies. My family donates to the poor and offers food at Thanksgiving because it's important to remember where one comes from and appreciate the abundance you might have.

4

10 years old QHHT

Throughout this book you are going to see me right about my experiences with QHHT. This is a practice that has both fascinated me and changed my life. During this piece of writing I am going to take you on a journey into a session where I was taken back to childhood.

I was 10 years old and in 4th grade. I traveled the hallways of my old school and could make out the colors of the walls. My practitioner who was conducting the session asked me to describe what was on the wall and I could clearly make out the poster that was placed on the wall conducting a poll of favorite T.V. shows.

It was 1994 and Full House was winning. I couldn't believe it; the memory had escaped me but instantly returned. I then continued to travel the hallway and made my way into the bathroom. Inside the bathroom I was brought to a scene that I remembered because at the time it traumatized me.

I had shut my friends' hand in the bathroom stall door inflicting pain upon him. In fear of getting in trouble I ran to the classroom where he followed and pinned me to the wall, pulling his fist back as if he was going to strike me. I was afraid.

I wasn't afraid of him exactly, but afraid of fighting him and hurting him. At the time I didn't realize how much this incident affected me, but it did. My practitioner asked me if there was anything I wanted to do or say during this scene. I apologized and it instantly made me feel amazing, and a feeling of closure.

I then moved to a scene where I was on the baseball field at the same school. I was in my white t-shit and white baseball pants. This was significant as I deeply enjoyed the sport and had given it up all too soon and missed it terribly.

I was a fantastic player having been on

multiple All-Star teams, school teams and making All Conference. I was playing catch with my dad. I could taste the dirt, and feel it filling my nostrils. I began to sob. The emotional turbulence was surreal but reliving the experience was priceless.

To feel as if I was 10 years old again was an amazing gift. And an experience that I will carry with me for the rest of my life. I am truly grateful.

A New Journey

Pondering your mind,

Escaping the burden of He,

He, the monster covered in a green mist.

Tucked away, surrounded in stain.

A beautiful taste of discomfort.

And your whole.

You have moved forward.

Working to fix oneself.

A journey to salvation from the past that

continues to haunt.

Lingering in mind,

A stitch in the soul.

For the tranquility of life,

Relaxes in the gaping hole.

Of soft beauty of breath.

And the wonders of youth escaping the life,

The younglings exploring the past.

You must go forth and move ahead with you soul.

And exist in both realms of purified touch.

Those that come to explain the path,

For you to follow and seek further control.

You will go and lay beneath the glow of the stars and kiss the energy of light.

Hello

Hello, are you there?

Can you hear me?

Or am I just wasting time asking you

questions?

Speaking into a microphone,

with you just fucking nodding on the other

line,

like a mute at a fucking drive in movie.

What's wrong?

Are you mad, or just don't give a shit about

me? The person on the other end of the line.

Shutting up only to wait for your turn to

speak.

Why do I even bother?

Do you realize it works both ways?

Well you reap what you sew when all is lost

in a line of communication.

Time Flies

Times sure goes by. Super quick. I mean I woke up and I was 35. However, it seems like yesterday I just turned 21. I have four beautiful children and will be celebrating 15 years of marriage soon. Time flies, but I guess who is counting?

I often try to think about my childhood and for some reason I can't remember a lot. I remember baseball, and the teenage years, but right now that is about it. I will write about that in an autobiographical piece I have planned soon as memories come back to me, however I am puzzled.

Time sure does go by though. I remember my children being born. That feeling will never leave me. Miracle's I tell you. Meeting my daughter Courtney at 5 months old, her little round face; precious. Seeing Mikayla be born and recognizing her from the silhouette. Caelyn coming out and looking so much like her mother and Courtney, and then Kenny, that was amazing.

The birth of my son, my namesake. And the ordeal we suffered with him. The fear of losing him and my wife due to placenta previa. That we will discuss later in this book. But god how time flies and I have cherished ever single minute of it. I love my family. I love my newfound existence. And

the journey my soul has taken.

5

Into the Sun.

The melting pot of dismay,

You on the other end of pure.

Encompassing my life as your own,

in order to fulfill some sort of fortune.

It must be your own because you gave witness,

For you did nothing,

But wallow in the distance.

No touch. No question, not even a handshake.

Just an eerie sign of utter disbelief in hopes I would not be left alone in the distance.

"How are you my dear"?

Is all you ask.

Then left alone to fend for oneself.

For you feel as if your job has been carried out.

A job well done.

When really the task of burden does not end,

Until the day you begin to parish, into the sun.

Maturity

Over the years I have developed into a writer. It has always been there but lately it has been more prevalent. I started in 5th grade where I would write horror stories and my teacher would allow me to read them to the class. I had black and white composition notebooks filled page after page with characters of gore and guts. Story after story all inspired by the Great R.L. Stein and the Feat Street series.

By all accounts I was a writer and that's what I originally wanted to be. So then when I was about 12 years old, I slowly started sinking into a deep and dark depression. I began to write poetry. Oh, how I loved the art of poetry. I was able to crawl out of my skin and release the angst from within through written words.

I would spill tears, and even blood, but boy those words would luminate the pages. And in a way saved me from my self. I wrote nonstop for ten years. That created the book "Confessions of a Boy with No Name". When writing that book, I could clearly see not only the sadness and suicidal ideation, but the maturity level change. I had grown.

I was such a scared little boy, living in

fear. Tears and would cower in the corner. The book spilled it all, it was and is a time capsule of my life, of my maturity and progression through the years.

I had attempted suicide in that book, joined the army, suffered emotional abuse, countless relationships and met my wife and daughter. I was alive in that book and because of that book, it felt good to be alive and still does.

There was a major gap after 2006. I felt that since I was better emotionally that I no longer needed to write, oh how wrong I was. I went through things and saw things. I had three more children in the time it took for me to write again. I knew it was time in 2012. You see before I put Confessions together there was "Suffering in Silence".

"Suffering in Silence" is and was something I am not proud of. It was my first attempt at putting something together with all my previous work, and newfound maturity level. However due to writing most of it in a manic state, my education level was misguided and translated onto paper inaccurately. I was ashamed.

In 2017 I put out Confessions, and then I was engaged in new material. My first new material in years. All that had built up for some time exploded and gave birth to

"The Monster and I" series volume 1-3. It was amazing. This time around my education level, my maturity, and my emotions were on point.

True I was in a hypo-manic state, however I was feeling the best I had in years. The words flowed and though I tackled some serious subjects, things I had hoped to forget. I felt elated.

As a writer I had grown, and my word choice and emotions were where they needed to be. As I write this, I realize I again have grown. This is so different from anything I have ever done. I have grown and expanded into something like no other. I feel that I am unstoppable.

I am sorry

Taken back to childhood,

Holding the picture of youth...

What do you say to the inner child?

His pain, his turmoil and eyes of burden.

Lead through intimidation and fear.

You yearn to hold him,

Telling him your sorry for what you have put

him through.

Though your past is his.

And he is you, living parallel through each

other.

What do you say?

I love you?

It will be ok.

You explore the remanence of his innocence,

And the blonde upon his crown.

Blue radiates his sight,

And the comfort of his arms you only dream

to feel.

You!

And he is both the same.

Again, I ask you. What do you say?

I am sorry, I am sorry.

Newfound Existence

I once walked with the monster on my

shoulder,

The burden of he,

Always lingering from within.

How I conquered his being and left him for

dead.

Occasionally he filters through,

But not today, nor tomorrow.

For I am ready. Growing and walking with

my head in the clouds.

A Newfound Existence

Smelling the refreshments of starlight,

The essence of soul,

The shell of those who surround us in their

ships,

Guiding us and ready for us to go.

The monster sits beside me,

But he is silenced.

Pills mute his voice,

But the S.C. has destroyed his will of power.

The White pyramid has taken me by the

hand,

Guiding me through the green mist,

And treated me from the internal source.

6

Dysphoric Mania Poetry Mumblings

Years ago

- I sit and feel a dark shadow begin to shade my face, I glace to see a dark cloud giving shelter to a disgraceful human being, warm fluid indents my cheeks, but its nots rain, its coming from my eyes.

-   And though I'm sitting alone it's getting harder to breath. In a desperate need for air and no where to get it. A light shine revealing a pleasure pistol. The temptation is there to place my hand upon its handle. Squeeze the trigger, closing my eyes and remove myself from this scene of the world.

-   Peering into a thought,

    Hoping to reveal true feelings of

    happiness, pleasure and pain but

    nothing exists.

\-   A melancholy scapegoat. A yearning, a
wanting to no longer to be alone.
There's a picture of you and its slowly
fading away.

Each days a determination to be free,
free from the grips of bipolar, escape
the feeling of sadness, mania and
mortal death.

-   Scared and uncovered,

    Ashamed and derailed,

    Forgive hopefully to forget.

    Pain with a mental picture of it.

    Deep behind my eyes of lasting

    suicide envy.

-Painted face

A sour distinctive taste.

A soul not worth selling,

A fragrance not worth smelling,

A permanent depressive stain,

A mind tormented filled with pain.

Wrist needs to be slit.

Create cancer keep my cigarette lit.

Suicide touch and become friends.

Erase my smile when love ends.

Slowly die.

Say goodbye.

Ashes to ashes.

Dust to dust.

Must go to hell.

If a must.

Kenneth

Our Son Kenneth (Kenny) was born May 6, 2012 at 31 weeks gestation (9 weeks) early. The pregnancy was both rewarding and traumatic as my wife Melissa had placenta previa. Due to the possibility of hemorrhaging we were not sure if both would survive the birth.

This led to a confliction in my heart, as if given a choice I wanted my wife, my heart my flame to survive; however, my baby, my flesh deserved a chance at life. I had no faith, nothing and felt all alone.

These were very scary times. A young father of three, with young kids; meanwhile they didn't understand why their mom lay in the hospital bed on bed rest for six long weeks. Looking to me for answers, I had no gall to tell them that she was trying to save two lives, hers and their brothers.

They were already scared, and it was my job to protect them. I spent my nights away from my wife, in mania. I lived off one hour of sleep, it was all I needed. My youngest daughter would cry herself to sleep on my chest each night. Yearning for her mother, at three years old she had no clue.

I was unmedicated and felt untouchable and in control, but really, I was a mess, decaying inside. Again, I was alone, with no support.

There were few who lent the occasional hand, but no one to sit and talk with. There was no conversation and no interaction. I was dying without my love, and it killed me knowing she was all alone in that hospital bed.

My wife is the most selfless person I know. She stayed in bed to protect our unborn son. She loved him immediately from the time he was conceived. She nurtured him in the womb, and she nearly lost her life the day she hemorrhaged and had her emergency caesarian section.

Kenny was born and instantly taken to

another room. I missed the birth by seconds but was able to rush to my wife's side as they stitched her up. I was relieved to see she was well. She instantly told me to check on our son, as she again was selfless neglecting herself.

I went and check on Kenny and they were hooking him up to monitors and putting tubes down his throat. I started to cry as this was a scary sight, as well as happy as I now had a son. I cried out his name and for a split second he opened his eyes. I captured that moment in a photograph. His eyes would remain shut for the duration of the day, but that moment will live in my heart forever.

After Kenny was born, I went into a major mental mixed episode. I had complete mental failure and was engulfed in multiple emotions all at once. I had kept myself guarded during the duration of the pregnancy and once that was open, it as if a wall had been taken down.

The lack of medication had got the best of me and I was truly learning what it meant to be untherapeutic. I went full blown manic, then into a depressive episode. I had paranoid delusions, the shadows of death and the worst was I had bouts of suicidal ideation.

With the paranoid delusions I

remember working inside the place of business I managed, and I would constantly look out the window in fear of men in black suits and ties coming to get me. I was miserable and I didn't know what to do. It was as if my body had relaxed from Kenny's birth being over and successful that my brain was beginning to cry out for help from the trauma it had suffered.

I went to the walk-in clinic for mental health at the nearby Veterans Administration Hospital. I remember saying that I couldn't get my brain to shut off and I needed their help. They immediately wanted to hospitalize me, but I did not allow that to happen. I instead was placed on new medication in a hope to begin the long journey to stability.

I was also told at this time that after being off medication for so long and then suffering through such a traumatic event, I can never be off meds again. As of this writing I have been on my medication for the past 7 years and am now stable and feeling the best I have since my diagnoses in 2003.

Who to Blame?

When the day settles and you look to the sky, Clinch your fist,

Who to blame?

Is it the he who lingered in the shadows,

Or the man from around the way?

How about that beauty by your side?

Or the child who looks to you for life.

Who to blame?

Sometimes it's hard,

But we must write our names,

Gift wrap them on the mistakes we
have made.

Traveling through the day. And chilling
amongst the decaying fields left behind.

Who to blame?

Look beside yourself and you reveal no one.

But when looking in the mirror, ask yourself,

who to blame...?

And your answer will be staring right back at you.

Now, who do you blame?

Bipolar and I, Essay

In 2003 I was diagnosed with Bipolar Affective disorder and later determined to be Bipolar type 1 with rapid cycle. At first it hit me like a ton of bricks because I didn't understand what was happening to me and I couldn't get a grip on the balance within my brain.

As the years went by and I became stable I grew determined to help others with this disorder as well as other mental illnesses. I learned that with will power and a good support system anything is possible. It is a part of what I am, but not who I am.

I am a husband, a father and an individual who is determined to take the hand they were dealt and do some good with it. If I can reach just one person, I will have succeeded. My family is everything to me, but I have also learned to love myself as well and have found that doing things for myself is not necessarily a bad thing. We all have demons, some more than others, I just have to continue the fight, we all do.

With Bipolar type 1 I also suffer from severe depressive episodes that mimics Bipolar type 2, Mania and Hypo Mania and Mixed Episodes. This illness is serious, but after 16+ years I feel I have a grip on it and basically am in what I call the maintenance phase. I am stable on my medicine and see my psychiatrist to stay up to date on everything.

You may wonder why I am doing this, and my answer is that it is for educational purposes. If more people were educated on the subject maybe there would be less misconception, less concern and more care out there for us. It seems like the mental health field always gets the shaft when it comes to funding, yet always gets blamed when it comes to crimes.

Bipolar type 1 is considered to be the most severe as we have the most drastic shifts in mood, going from extreme Mania into depression, and at times both (Mixed). As I have written in my poetry I have been to the depths of hell. Bipolar takes patience and a good healthy support system, all of which I have. It took many years to get to where I am and many medications along the way.

I challenge anyone who may disagree with my words as I live with this daily. I might be on medication for the rest of my life; however, I will not let this prevent me from living a normal life. With regards, always keeping the monster at bay.

In Closing

Overcoming and Growing

I have battled many things in my life. From adolescent depression to severe depression, to bipolar disorder and anxiety. I have become a husband and a father. I have emotionally been hurt, and emotionally hurt the ones I love.

But I am a survivor. I am a lover of all people and a protector of my family. In my years I have grown to realize that it's a "live and let live" kind of world; or at least it should be. Why inflict pain and suffering and torment onto others, or wish ill will? We should band together and work to make our world better.

We are derived from energy. Now whether you believe in a particular religion or faith, you can't argue that our vessels or vehicles we walk around in are derived from energy. Energy feeds off energy and it is up to us what we do with that energy.

Through QHHT, self-discovery and my writing, I have healed and started to grow to love myself. I am no longer the sad and lonely little boy in "Confessions of a Boy with no Name", but in fact a man for whom has survived.

I have picked up that bottle of pills and swallowed, I did place a gun to my head. But that was not part of the contract I signed up for when my energy decided to come here. And that is why I am here today. I am not just a man who lives with mental illness. I am a person with a story and a message. I encourage you to find your story and your message as well.

In closing I leave you with this thought. What if you were sent here to learn as much as there is that you possibly need to learn. Maybe you had a past life where a lesson was not learned and therefore in this life you must learn it. In order to move on to the that "better place" you must clear that karma. Would you live your life any different?

Thank you.

KENNETH J CODY

ABOUT THE AUTHOR

Kenneth J Cody was born in Chesapeake Virginia and grew up in Currituck North Carolina. He spent his high school years in and around Annapolis Maryland and joined the United States Army at the age 17 in 2001.

While in the Army Kenneth sustained a back injury as well as being diagnosed with bipolar disorder type 1, leaving him a non-combat service-connected disabled veteran. He was honorably discharged in 2003. Over the years Kenneth has developed a love for helping other veterans and their families becoming an advocate for mental health.

Kenneth now resides in Florida with his wife Melissa and their four children. Holding a BA in Psychology/ Human Resource Management, he hopes to one day finish his Masters in English with a focus on Poetry.